Length

Length	English	Metric	Verse
Finger	0.73 in.	1.85 cm.	Jeremiah 52.21
Handbreadth (4 fingers)	2.92 in.	7.4 cm.	Exodus 25:25
Span	9 in.	22.86 cm.	Exodus 28:16
Cubit	18 in.	45.72 cm.	Matthew 6:27
Long Cubit	20.4 in.	51.9 cm.	Ezekiel 40:5
Fathom	6 ft.	1.829 m	Acts 27:28
Reed (6 cubits)	8.75 ft.	2.73 m	Ezekiel 40:5
Furlong	660 ft.	201.2 m	Revelation 14:20
Stadion	697 ft.	185.4 m	Luke 24:13
Sabbath Day's Journey	3/5 mi.	0.9656 km.	Acts 1:12
Day's journey	20 mi.	32.19 km.	1 Kings 19:4

Weights

Weights	English	Metric	Verse
Gerah	1/50 oz.	0.567 g	Ezekiel 45:12
Bekah (10 gerahs)	1/5 oz.	5.67 g	Genesis 24:22
Pim (2/3 shekel)	1/3 oz.	9.45 g	1 Samuel 13.21
Shekel (2 bekahs)	2/5 oz.	11.34 g	Exodus 30:23
Mina (50 shekels)	1.25 lbs.	0.567 kg.	Ezra 2:69
Talent (60 minas)	75 lbs.	34.02 kg.	Ezra 8:26

Liquid Measures

Liquid	Englis	Metric	Verse
Log	0.65 pt.	0.31 l.	Leviticus 14:10
Kab (4 logs)	2.6 pt.	1.2 l.	2 Kings 6:25
Hin (12 logs)	0.98 gal.	3.7 l.	Numbers 15:4
Bath (6 hins)	5.9 gal.	22 l.	Isaiah 5:10
Homer (10 baths)	59 gal.	220 l.	Ezekiel 45:11
Kor (10 baths)	59 gal.	220 l.	Ezekiel 45:11
Metretes	10 gal.	37.85 l.	John 2:6

Dry Measures

Measurement	English	Metric	Verse
Kab (1/18 ephah)	2.6 pt.	1.2 l.	2 Kings 6:25
Omer (1/10 ephah)	2.3 qt.	2.2 l.	Exodus 16:36
Seah (1/3 ephah)	7.7 qt.	7.3 l.	2 Kings 7:1
Ephah (10 omers)	5.9 gal.	22 l.	Ruth 2:17
Lethech (5 ephaths)	29 gal.	110 l.	Hosea 3:2
Homer (10 ephaths)	59 gal.	220 l.	Leviticus 27:16
Kor (10 ephaths)	59 gal.	220 l.	Ezekiel 45:14

Money

Money	English	Metric	Verse
Denarius (silver)	Day's Pay	Day's Pay	Matthew 20:2
Drachma (silver)	0.035 oz.	1 g	Luke 15:8
Didrachma (silver)	0.07 oz.	2 g	Matthew 17:24
Talent (silver)	50/100 lbs	45.4 kg	Ezra 8:26
Talent (gold)	60/120 lbs	54.4 kg	1 Kings 9:28

Time

Time	Standard	Military	Verse
Sunrise	6 AM	06:00	Mark 16:2
First hour	7 AM	07:00	-
Second hour	8 AM	08:00	-
Third hour	9 AM	09:00	Matthew 20:3
Fourth hour	10 AM	10:00	-
Fifth hour	11 AM	11:00	-
Sixth hour	12 PM	12:00	Matthew 27:45
Seventh hour	1 PM	13:00	John 4:52
Eighth hour	2 PM	14:00	-
Ninth hour	3 PM	15:00	Acts 3:1
Tenth hour	4 PM	16:00	John 1:39
Eleventh hour	5 PM	17:00	Matthew 20:6-9
Sunset	6 PM	18:00	Luke 4:40

First watch of night	6 PM - 9 PM	18:00 - 21:00	-
Second watch	9 PM - midnight	21:00 - 00:00	Luke 12:38
Third watch	Midnight - 3 AM	00:00 - 03:00	Luke 12:38
Fourth watch	3 AM - 6 AM	03:00 - 06:00	Matthew 14:25

Misc. Weights and Measures

_____

_____

_____

_____

_____

_____

_____

_____

_____

_____

_____

_____

The 48 Laws of Black Empowerment

The 48 Laws of Power was written by Robert Greene and first published in 1998. It is often praised as one of the best books to read if you want to get ahead in life. This got me to thinking, "why isn't there anything like this for our community?"

We have a lot of people talking about what we need to do, what we should do, and what we could do as a community, but nothing concrete that we could all sit down with, learn from, and relate to on an individual level. The 48 Laws of Black Empowerment was written to bridge the gap between individual action and a united black community. This book is broken down into six areas of importance to the black community.

1. Personal
2. Family
3. Finance
4. Community
5. Activism

Working to individually improve ourselves in these areas will automatically result in a shift in black community consciousness. While The 48 Laws of Power is a great book, it just wasn't written with our community or needs in mind. The 48 Laws of Black Empowerment is about cultivating success in business and life, while also helping our friends, family and community succeed with us.

Scan the QR code to buy this book on Amazon or search for "The 48 Laws of Black Empowerment."

Support Black Businesses

Bible Study Bookz

Notebooks With Covers That Represent Our Culture

Bible Study Bookz are lined notebooks that are perfect for the Bible study enthusiast that loves to take notes and keep them. Each notebook includes the following tables to enhance your study time.

- Biblical Lengths
- Biblical Weights
- Biblical Liquid Measures
- Biblical Dry Measures
- Biblical Money
- Biblical Time

Each book is compact, which makes it perfect for travel, and Bible Study Bookz can be stored on any bookshelf for easy keeping.

Available On Amazon

The Awakening Initiative

Thank you for reading The Black Hebrew Awakening. In an effort to awaken more of our people, I'm stealing a play from The Negro Project. Every month I'm going to send an Awakening Box to the pastors of ten black churches. The goal is to awaken the pastor so that the pastor can awaken the congregation. If you would like to help me reach more than ten pastors per month, please visit my Patreon page to read more about The Awakening Initiative.

The Awakening Box

patreon.com/dantefortson

Please Leave A Five Star Review

If you enjoyed reading this book, please leave a five star review on Amazon. Your review is important because it helps our people decide if they want to buy the book. If you believe what is written in this book is important, please take a few moments to leave a review. Thanks in advance.

Made in the USA
Middletown, DE
24 September 2023

39173432R00056